better together*

*This book is best read together, grownup and kid.

akidsbookabout.com

a kids book about™

FEMINISM

by Emma Mcilroy

a kids book about™

Library of Congress Cataloging-in-Publication Data is available.

This book represents my personal experience and thus is not intended to be representative of every form or example of feminism.

A Kids Book About Feminism is exclusively available online on the a kids book about website.

To share your stories, ask questions, or inquire about bulk purchases (schools, libraries, and non-profits), please use the following email address:

hello@akidsbookabout.com

www.akidsbookabout.com

ISBN: 978-1-951253-02-8

Printed in the USA

For Caroline, Daniel & John -
May the future be feminist

Intro

When you hear a little boy say, "Boys are better than girls," it's more than just a frivilous statement. We are so conditioned to sexism that we sometimes forget it exists at all or act like it's harmless. It's not.

So how do we change this?

Believe it or not, feminism is the answer. I know, "The F-Word" can sound really intimidating. But this book is on a mission to make feminism not only accessible to every girl and boy, but also something they aspire to embrace.

Buckle up, and hopefully by the end of this book, you'll call yourself a feminist too!

Hi, my name is Emma.

I'm from Belfast, a city on the top part of Ireland.

I'm a CEO.

I'm a woman.

And I'm a feminist.

Feminism is
SUPER COOL

And guess what?

You can be a feminist, too.

And if you choose to be one,

YOU CAN CHANGE THE WORLD.

Some people think feminism is scary.

Some people think only women can be feminists.

Some people think feminists don't like boys.

But that's not true.

Feminism is the belief that...

EVERYONE IS EQUAL NO MATTER WHAT THEIR GENDER IS.

1.

Feminists believe everybody should be treated the same way.

2.

Feminists believe that just because you're a girl doesn't mean you are less valuable.

3.

Feminists believe everybody should have the same opportunities.

4.

Feminists want the world to be a better place for everyone.

DO YOU AGREE?

Sometimes people treat girls differently...

right?

Some people think girls...

Can't do math

Aren't good at science

Should be skinny

Always look pretty

Can't be doctors

Have to get married

Should make less money

Some people think boys are...

Better

Stronger

Smarter

Faster

More capable

But...

THAT'S NONSENSE!

BONKERS!!
BANANAS!!!

Let me tell you the...

TRUTH!

GIRLS CAN WIN THE WORLD CUP!

Just ask Megan Rapinoe.

GIRLS

CAN

RUN BIG

COMPANIES!

Like Pepsi, ever heard of it?

GIRLS CAN WIN NOBEL PRIZES!

Like Malala at 17 years old.

GIRLS CAN BE PRESIDENT!

Like in Brazil and Ireland.

It's SUPER important you're
a feminist, too...

EVEN IF YOU'R

NOT A GIRL.

Because there are so many things that have to...

NGE

Like when you hear someone say...

Only boys can...

That's not for girls...

Girls can't...

Boys are better at...

Remember, that's NOT TRUE!

And tell them that you know a girl who...

WON THE
NOBEL PRIZE!

And ladies...

BE
ACCEPT
LOVE
APPRECIATE

YOURSELF.

YOURSELF.

YOURSELF.

YOURSELF.

Because we think you're

AWES

OME!!

I'm a feminist, and I want to fight for all women...

NO MATTER...

What their skin color is,

Which country they're from,

Who they choose to love,

What body parts they have,

How much money they make,

Or what they choose to wear.

Because when we fight for everyone

AND

give them the same opportunities...

the world gets better for...

ALL OF US.

Outro

Alright, that was pretty intense, huh? Good, because treating everyone equally is a PRETTY INTENSE matter.

Everyone is equal, so everyone should be treated equally. And if you believe that, guess what?

YOU'RE A FEMINIST!

I'd like to be the first to welcome you and that kiddo with you to the club.

You are a part of a movement that's made up of fellow rascals, rule breakers, think-out-of-the-boxers, and world changers. The only criteria for belonging? Believe that everyone should be treated equally!

Whatever you do, don't let that belief stop with this book. Bring it with you everywhere you go, because you know the same thing I do: Everyone is equal.

find
more
kids
books
about

racism, belonging, creativity, money, depression, failure, gratitude, adventure, cancer, body image, and mindfulness.

akidsbookabout.com

share your read*

*Tell somebody, post a photo, or give this book away to share what you care about.

@akidsbookabout